World War II

Lisa Zamosky and Wendy Conklin, M.A.

Publishing Credits

Historical Consultant
Shannon C. McCutchen

Editor
Torrey Maloof

Editorial Director
Emily R. Smith, M.A.Ed.

Editor-in-Chief
Sharon Coan, M.S.Ed.

Creative Director
Lee Aucoin

Illustration Manager
Timothy J. Bradley

Publisher
Rachelle Cracchiolo, M.S.Ed.

Teacher Created Materials
5301 Oceanus Drive
Huntington Beach, CA 92649-1030
http://www.tcmpub.com

ISBN 978-0-7439-0668-5

Table of Contents

Secret Missions and Superbombs

December 7, 1941, started out like any other quiet Sunday in Hawaii. People were getting out of bed and starting their days. Suddenly, the world changed forever. Hundreds of Japanese airplanes started bombing the U.S. military base at Pearl Harbor. The terrible surprise attack lasted for almost two hours. More than 2,400 people were killed. And, almost 1,200 more were wounded.

Before this day, the war in Europe seemed far away to people in the United States. But World War II was not just fought in Europe.

There was an enemy in the Pacific, too. When, the Japanese attacked Pearl Harbor that day, it shocked the world.

For Americans, this day pushed them into a deadly war. For the world, it sparked the beginning of a **nuclear** (NOO-klee-uhr) era. Scientists created bombs that destroyed entire cities. These superbombs spared no one, including innocent (IN-nuh-suhnt) children. World War II was an ugly, vicious war. It changed millions of lives around the world.

Just an Intermission

Some historians say that World War II was a continuation of World War I. There was just a long intermission in between!

Mad After World War I

Japan fought with the Allies during World War I. After that war, Japanese leaders were angry about the peace agreement. The leaders did not gain much territory. They wanted to make Japan a major world power.

After the attack, five battleships were sunk. Three others were damaged. And, many other ships needed repair.

The Japanese emperor, Hirohito (hear-oh-HEE-tow), led Japan into a war against the United States.

How the War Began

Adolf Hitler was the leader of **Nazi** (NOT-see) Germany. He wanted to make Germany bigger. In 1938, he announced a plan. He merged his homeland of Austria with Germany. Soon, Nazi flags flew all over Austria.

Then, Hitler decided to take over Czechoslovakia (chek-uh-slow-VAW-kee-uh). He printed lies in German newspapers saying that Germans were treated badly in that country. He reminded the public that before World War I, Czechoslovakia was part of Germany. No one objected, so his army took over that country, too.

Hitler wanted to take over all of Europe, and it seemed the world was going to let him do it. He planned to attack Poland next. This time, both Great Britain and France objected. They warned him that this would start a war, but Hitler believed they would not stop him.

On September 1, 1939, Hitler invaded Poland, and World War II began. Hitler destroyed the Polish capital. He hoped that this easy victory would scare the British and French. Hitler offered them a chance for peace. They refused. This time, Hitler had gone too far.

Switching Sides

When Germany invaded Poland from the west, the Soviet Union invaded it from the east. But in June 1941, Germany invaded the Soviet Union. The Soviet leader, Joseph Stalin, switched sides in the war. The Soviets started fighting with the Allied forces against Germany.

Other World Leaders

Hitler was not the only leader who wanted to rule the world. Other men like Emperor Hirohito in Japan and Benito Mussolini (buh-NEE-tow moos-suh-LEE-nee) in Italy felt the same. Hitler and these leaders formed a **pact**. They were the leaders of the Axis powers.

Benito Mussolini led Italy during World War II.

Adolf Hitler was an emotional and powerful speaker. This helped him gain control in Germany.

The New York Times on September 1, 1939

"All the News That's Fit to Print."

The New York Times.

EXTRA
Partly cloudy and somewhat warmer today. Tomorrow generally fair with moderate temperatures.
Temperatures Yesterday—Max., 67; Min., 61

Copyright, 1939, by The New York Times Company.

VOL. LXXXVIII...No. 29,805. Entered as Second-Class Matter, Postoffice, New York, N. Y. NEW YORK, FRIDAY, SEPTEMBER 1, 1939. THREE CENTS New York City and Vicinity | FOUR CENTS Elsewhere Except in 7th and 8th Postal Zones.

GERMAN ARMY ATTACKS POLAND; CITIES BOMBED, PORT BLOCKADED; DANZIG IS ACCEPTED INTO REICH

BRITISH MOBILIZING

Navy Raised to Its Full Strength, Army and Air Reserves Called Up

PARLIAMENT IS CONVOKED

Midnight Meeting Is Held by Ministers—Negotiations Admitted Failure

By The Associated Press.

LONDON, Friday, Sept. 1.—The British Parliament was summoned to meet today at 5 P. M. [12 noon in New York].

British Call Up Forces

By FERDINAND KUHN Jr.
Special Cable to THE NEW YORK TIMES.

LONDON, Friday, Sept. 1.—All attempts to bring about direct negotiations between Germany and Poland appeared to have broken down tonight as Great Britain mobilized her fleet to full strength, stretched her other defensive preparations close to the limit and began moving 3,000,000 school children and invalids from the crowded cities into the safety of the countryside.

Censorship was established over cables after London had been cut off for hours from communication with the Continent.

It was the peak of the crisis, but a day of rumors had not shifted the fundamental issue nor given a conclusive answer to the question of peace or war.

At midnight the British Government was not yet convinced that Germany really intended to attack Poland and provoke a world war.

Terms Called Smoke Screen

All that had happened during yesterday, including the sudden broadcasting of Chancellor Hitler's sixteen-point demands, was interpreted here as a smoke screen rather than as the flash of guns.

After hearing Herr Hitler's "terms" officials here quietly announced tonight that "the government primarily interested in the proposals is, of course, the Polish Government."

Until the Polish Government has had time to consider them, it was said in Whitehall that "it would be highly undesirable for any com-

Bulletins on Europe's Conflict

London Hears of Warsaw Bombing

LONDON, Friday, Sept. 1 (AP).—Reuters British news agency said it had learned from Polish sources in Paris that Warsaw was bombed today.

French Confirm Beginning of War

PARIS, Friday, Sept. 1 (AP).—The Havas news agency said today that official French dispatches from Germany indicated that "the Reich began hostilities on Poland this morning."

The agency also reported that the Polish Embassy here had announced that "Germany violated the Polish frontier at four points."

"German reports of pretended violation of German territory by Poland are pure invention, as is the fable of 'attack' by Polish insurgents on Gleiwitz," the embassy announcement said.

Attack on Entire Front Reported

LONDON, Friday, Sept. 1 (AP).—A Reuters dispatch from Paris said:

"The following is given with all reserve: According to unconfirmed reports received here, the Germans have begun an offensive with extreme violence on the whole Polish front."

First Wounded Brought Into Gleiwitz

GLEIWITZ, Germany, Friday, Sept. 1 (AP).—An army ambulance carrying wounded soldiers arrived at the emergency hospital here today at 9:10 A. M.

The men, carried in a wagon, were on stretchers. One had on a first-aid field bandage. It could not be ascertained where the ambulance came from.

At about 9:30 a half-mile long truck train manned by the engineering corps drove through the heart of the city with pontoon bridge building material. In the train were caterpillar tread, twenty-passenger motor vans.

Obviously the train had been on the road for a considerable time. All equipment was thickly covered with gray mud.

A scouting plane of the air force was patrolling an area over Gleiwitz.

Early today Gleiwitz residents reported that artillery fire

Continued on Page Four

DALADIER SUMMONS CABINET TO CONFER

News of Attack on Poland Spurs Prompt Action—Military Move Thought Likely

By The Associated Press.

PARIS, Friday, Sept. 1.—Edouard Daladier, Premier and War Minister of France, informed that Ger-

BRITISH CHILDREN TAKEN FROM CITIES

3,000,000 Persons Are in First Evacuation Group, Which Is to Be Moved Today

By FREDERICK T. BIRCHALL
Special Cable to THE NEW YORK TIMES.

LONDON, Friday, Sept. 1.—The greatest mass movement of popula-

HOSTILITIES BEGUN

Warsaw Reports German Offensive Moving on Three Objectives

ROOSEVELT WARNS NAVY

Also Notifies Army Leaders of Warfare—Envoys Tell of Bombing of 4 Cities

By JERZY SZAPIRO
Wireless to THE NEW YORK TIMES.

WARSAW, Poland, Friday, Sept. 1.—War began at 5 o'clock this morning with German planes attacking Gdynia, Cracow and Katowice.

At Gdynia three bombs exploded in the sea.

The regular German Army started an offensive in the direction of Dzialdowka—in Upper Silesia and Czestochowa. The German plan apparently is to cut off Western Poland along the line of Dzialdowka-Lodz-Czestochowa.

The offensive is developing, from East Prussia, toward Silesia and northwards from Slovakia.

At 9 o'clock an attempt was made to bombard Warsaw. The planes, however, did not reach even the suburbs.

A military attack on the garrison at Westerplatte in the Danzig area was repulsed.

The Foreign Office at 8:45 A. M. issued a communiqué saying that military action had begun in Westerplatte in the Danzig area as well as in Buschkowa near Gdynia, and in Dzialowka, Chojnice and Lowa.

Hostilities have begun and Poland has been attacked, said the communiqué.

Three cities in Upper Silesia suffered artillery bombardment, particulars of which are lacking, it was said.

While this dispatch was being telephoned, the air-raid sirens sounded in Warsaw.

Danzig Fighting Reported

WARSAW, Poland, Friday, Sept. 1 (AP).—It was reported today that Tczew and Czestochowa were bombed by German airplanes early this morning.

There was no official confirmation of the bombing.

FREE CITY IS SEIZED

Forster Notifies Hitler of Order Putting Danzig Into the Reich

ACCEPTED BY CHANCELLOR

Poles Ready, Made Their Preparations After Hostilities Appeared Inevitable

DANZIG, Friday, Sept. 1.—By a decree issued early this morning Albert Forster, Nazi Chief of State, proclaimed the annexation of the Free City to the Reich, thus settling by a fell stroke the original point of contention in the international crisis.

In a telegram to Chancellor Hitler Herr Forster explained his action as necessary to remove "the pressing necessity of our people and State." Herr Forster also issued a proclamation to the people of Danzig saying the hour awaited for twenty years had arrived because "our Fuehrer, Adolf Hitler, has freed us."

[A NEW YORK TIMES dispatch from Berlin this morning said Herr Hitler telegraphed Herr Forster today thanking him and all Danzigers, and stating:

"The law for reannexation is in effect immediately."

The Chancellor stated, furthermore, that Herr Forster was appointed head of the civil administration of the Danzig area.]

In a four-article decree Herr Forster declared the Constitution of Danzig no longer valid. He declared himself sole administrator of the Danzig part of the German Reich, and he declared that until the Reich's legal system had been introduced by command of Herr Hitler all laws except the Constitution remained in effect. Then Herr Forster immediately wired Herr Hitler of his action, begged the Chancellor to give his approval of the move and through Reich law complete the annexation.

The German flag is now flying everywhere over Danzig, Herr Forster said, and all church bells resound to the event. "We thank God," he declared, "that He gave the Fuehrer the strength and the

Hitler Acts Against Poland

The port of Gdynia, north of Danzig (toward top of map), was blockaded this morning. At Gleiwitz (shown by cross) artillery fire was heard after a Polish-German skirmish had been reported there. Cracow, to the east, was among Polish cities said to have been bombed.

Hitler Tells the Reichstag 'Bomb Will Be Met by Bomb'

Chancellor Vows 'Fight Until Resolution' Against Poland—Gives Order of Succession As Goering, Hess, Then Senate to Choose

Chancellor Adolf Hitler of Germany, in a world broadcast this morning, opened "a fight until the resolution of the situation" against Poland, announcing that "from now on bomb will be met by bomb."

bers had been awaiting the signal, and when the opera house opened shortly before 10 o'clock [5 o'clock, New York time] this morning, they were dressed in the uniforms of their military formations.

HITLER GIVES WORD

In a Proclamation He Accuses Warsaw of Appeal to Arms

FOREIGNERS ARE WARNED

They Remain in Poland at Own Risk—Nazis to Shoot at Any Planes Flying Over Reich

By OTTO D. TOLISCHUS
Special Cable to THE NEW YORK TIMES.

BERLIN, Friday, Sept. 1.—Charging that Germany had been attacked, Chancellor Hitler at 5:11 o'clock this morning issued a proclamation to the army declaring that from now on force will be met with force and calling on the armed forces "to fulfill their duty to the end."

The text of the proclamation reads:

To the defense forces:

The Polish nation refused my efforts for a peaceful regulation of neighborly relations; instead it has appealed to weapons.

Germans in Poland are persecuted with a bloody terror and are driven from their homes. The series of border violations, which are unbearable to a great power, prove that the Poles no longer are willing to respect the German frontier. In order to put an end to this frantic activity no other means is left to me now than to meet force with force.

"Battle for Honor"

German defense forces will carry on the battle for the honor of the living rights of the reawakened German people with firm determination.

I expect every German soldier, in view of the great tradition of eternal German soldiery, to do his duty until the end.

Remember always in all situations you are the representatives of National Socialist Greater Germany!

Long live our people and our Reich!

Berlin, Sept. 1, 1939.

ADOLF HITLER.

Why Stay Out of the War?

People today may wonder why the United States stayed out of the war at first. After all, the United States helped Great Britain and France win World War I. And, the United States believed in democracy. So why were they not alarmed when **dictators** (DIK-tay-terz) like Hitler came to power?

In fact, many Americans were alarmed by these dictators. But, some leaders in Congress felt the United States should stay out of all wars. These people were **pacifists** (PASS-uh-fistz). They felt that their good example would encourage others to support peace. Others felt the United States should keep to itself. They did not want to get involved in another European war. They were known as **isolationists** (i-suh-LAY-shun-istz). They did not think it was important to keep a strong military.

However, President Franklin Roosevelt disagreed. He worried about dictators like Hitler. The United States had let its army shrink. Roosevelt knew he had to build up the military to defend the United States. He was not about to let dictators take over his free country.

Isolationists speak to members of Congress. They did not want the United States to go to war.

The Nazi salute was used by the Nazi Party as a sign of loyalty to its leader, Adolf Hitler.

Lend-Lease Program

The United States sent Great Britain and its allies weapons and other materials. This was part of the Lend-Lease Program. And, President Roosevelt wanted an army to be ready just in case. So, the U.S. Congress started a **draft** to raise an army.

Antiwar Leader

Jeannette Rankin was the first U.S. congresswoman. She was a pacifist who did not believe the United States should go to war. She made headlines in 1916 when she voted against the United States entering World War I. After the attack on Pearl Harbor, Rankin once again voted against war. She said, "As a woman I can't go to war, and I refuse to send anyone else." She was the only member of Congress to vote against the war.

The Fight in Europe

The Germans used a tactic called **blitzkrieg** (BLITS-kreeg), or lightning war, against the British and French. The plan was that first German planes would drop many bombs on the enemies. Then, the German army would move in with tanks. This blitzkrieg caught Great Britain and France by surprise. The Germans started by bombing British aircraft factories and airfields. In just two weeks, the Allies were on the run. France had to **surrender** (suh-REN-duhr). Hitler knew that only Great Britain stood in his way of ruling Europe. Hitler offered the British a deal. Their leader, Winston Churchill, refused. And, the Battle of Britain began.

Battles took place in the sky between German and British planes. Night after night, the Germans dropped bombs on British cities. More than 40,000 British people died. But knowing they were the last hope, the British refused to give in. By May 1941, Hitler knew he had lost the Battle of Britain. Hitler's planes could not keep up with Churchill's Royal Air Force. For the time being, Hitler had to give up his plans to rule Great Britain.

Allies vs. Axis Powers

There were two sides in World War II. Germany, Italy, and Japan were on one side. They were known as the Axis powers. On the other side were Great Britain and France. Together these countries were known as the Allies. The Soviet Union and United States would join the Allies later in the war.

Hitler's Symbol

In 1920, Hitler said that the Nazi Party needed its own flag. On it, he chose to place the symbol of a **swastika** (SWAWS-tih-kuh). It is a very old symbol. Before the Nazis used it, it meant life, good luck, and power.

Fighter pilots could identify German planes by the thick crosses that were painted on their aircrafts.

London suffered heavy damages from German air raids.

Sir Winston Churchill, his son Randolph, and his grandson Winston

Hitler's Terrible Decisions

Meanwhile, Hitler's victories throughout Europe brought fear to people all over the world. In the German-controlled countries, every Jewish person had to wear the **Star of David**. That made it easier for Hitler's secret police to round them up and move them to **ghettos** (GET-toez). The ghettos were crowded with more people streaming in day after day. Food was scarce. Many Jewish people died of starvation. They needed help, but no one came.

Eventually, Hitler started to send Jewish people to **concentration** (kon-suhn-TRAY-shuhn) **camps**. The Nazis separated husbands from wives and children. The prisoners had to work to save their lives. Many people died from exhaustion or starvation. If prisoners were too weak or sick to work, they were killed. In some camps, called death camps, people were murdered without getting the chance to work. Almost six million Jewish people died in these horrible camps.

On the war front, Hitler made a new plan of attack. He decided to attack the Soviet Union. This was in June 1941. Hitler felt that a Soviet defeat would show Great Britain that Germany was unstoppable.

Hitler thought the Soviets would give up easily. But the Nazi army failed to defeat them before the harsh winter arrived. The terrible fighting continued throughout 1942. In September 1942, the Nazis attacked Stalingrad (STAW-luhn-grad), a Soviet city. The Nazis won, but their army had no protection. The Soviets surrounded the city and trapped the German soldiers.

Concentration camp survivors

Attacking the Soviets

Some of Hitler's officers thought that attacking the Soviets was a bad decision. It expanded the war to two fronts. That means they were fighting in two different areas of the world. But no one was willing to stand up to Hitler and tell him he was wrong.

Joseph Stalin led the Soviets in the war.

German prisoners are marched through the streets of Stalingrad after their defeat in February 1943.

Stalingrad Prisoners

At Stalingrad, 91,000 Germans surrendered to the Soviets. As many as 85,000 of them died in Soviet prison camps.

The Navajo Code Talkers

The United States needed a good **code** during the war. The Navajo (NAH-vuh-ho) Indians had a unique language. It had been passed down for generations. The U.S. Marines asked Navajos to invent a code based on their language. No enemies ever broke this code. Here are a few sample words in the Navajo code:

bomber plane—jay-sho
company—nakia
Germany—besh-be-cha-he
major—che-chil-be-tah-ola
submarine—besh-lo

Secret Codes

In the 1940s, wireless radios were used by the armies to send messages. But, enemy troops could hear these messages. The Navajo code talkers could use these radios with their special code. No one could figure out what they were saying. On the other hand, the United States had figured out Japanese codes.

Two U.S. Marine Navajo code talkers send a radio transmission in 1943

Over in Japan

In 1937, Japan invaded China. That made the United States both worried and angry. The United States wanted Japan to pull out of China. President Roosevelt told Japanese leaders that the United States would not trade oil or steel with them anymore. This kept Japan from buying the supplies it needed to fight this war.

Japan really needed oil. The U.S. oil **embargo** (im-BAWR-go) caused problems for Japan. So, Japan decided to take over other nations in East Asia to supply the needed oil. Roosevelt knew the Japanese would do this. So, he stationed bomber planes in the Philippines. The Philippines stood between Japan and the nations with the oil they needed. The president also sent ships to a base in the Pacific Ocean. This base was Pearl Harbor in Hawaii. These actions by the United States frustrated the Japanese.

On December 2, 1941, the United States government sent a message to military leaders. They had **deciphered** (dih-SY-furd) a Japanese message. It said that the Japanese were planning an attack in the Pacific. No one realized this attack would happen at Pearl Harbor. Everyone thought it would be in Asia.

There were many fires in the city of Shanghai, China, after being bombed by the Japanese.

"This Is Not a Drill!"

Early on Sunday, December 7, 1941, hundreds of Japanese planes waited on ships in the Pacific Ocean. The Japanese wanted to attack at just the right moment to cause the most damage. Their plans were to bomb eight battleships and many grounded airplanes. Their target was Pearl Harbor, a naval (NAY-vuhl) base in Hawaii. About 50,000 American troops worked on the fleet of ships there. This was the biggest group of U.S. forces in the Pacific Ocean.

The first wave of Japanese fighter planes began bombing just before 8:00 A.M. A second wave of fighter planes arrived around 8:30 A.M. The men on the ground tried to shoot back. A few U.S. pilots managed to get planes into the air and fight. However, only about 29 Japanese planes were lost. On the other hand, U.S. losses included 188 aircraft and 21 ships. The Japanese bombs caused terrible damage and killed more than 2,400 Americans. The entire attack on Pearl Harbor lasted just under two hours.

Decoders in Washington, D.C., had figured out that an attack was coming. But, they did not realize it would happen in Pearl Harbor until it was too late. A telegraph from Washington warned, "This is not a drill!" The telegraph arrived after the attack was over.

What Did Roosevelt Know?

Some people wonder if Roosevelt knew Pearl Harbor would be attacked ahead of time. One thing is for sure, this attack helped get isolationists to see the need for war.

Rosie the Riveter

With so many men fighting the war, there was a need for new factory workers. The government started putting out posters asking women to join the workforce. "Rosie the Riveter" was the most popular of these posters. "Rosie" appears as a strong American woman ready to help.

War! War! War!

Japan saw its attack on Pearl Harbor as a success. They wanted it to be a surprise, and it was. On the same day, Japan also attacked six other British and U.S. bases. The Philippines was one of these bases. Japan hoped to completely knock the United States out of the Pacific.

But, the Japanese made some big mistakes that day. They did not bomb three major U.S. aircraft carriers as well as important oil storage tanks. Because these items survived the attack, the United States could still fight back. Today, it seems that Japan's biggest mistake was attacking in the first place. Revenge is a powerful motivator. It united Americans against Japan.

After Pearl Harbor, it seemed everyone was eager to declare war. The very next day, the United States and Great Britain declared war on Japan. Only three days later, Germany and Italy declared war on the United States.

Transport ships like these carried American troops in the Pacific.

What Is *Infamy*?

President Roosevelt called Pearl Harbor "a date which will live in infamy." He meant that it was a horrible day that people will never forget.

A Sleeping Giant

The commander of the Japanese navy worried about the Pearl Harbor attack. He said, "I fear all we have done is awaken a sleeping giant." He was afraid that the United States would declare war on Japan. He was right.

An Army of American Women

Over 150,000 American women joined the army during World War II. Although these women were not allowed to fight in the war, they held many important jobs. Some women were weather forecasters, war photographers, or mechanics. Others worked as control tower operators, parachute riggers, or crewmembers on training flights.

This photo shows the destroyer USS *Shaw* exploding during the Japanese raid on Pearl Harbor.

Internment Camps

After Pearl Harbor, a sad thing happened to some Japanese Americans. Armed guards forced them to leave their jobs, homes, and families. Guards were ordered to place them into camps. In all, there were about 110,000 people sent to War Relocation Centers. These camps are also called **internment** (in-TERN-muhnt) **camps**. About two-thirds of the people sent to these camps were Japanese American **citizens**. They were forced to live behind barbed wire fences. They had **inadequate** (in-AD-uh-kwuht) housing. Many prisoners died because they did not have doctors to tend to them.

The most shocking fact of all is that this happened on American soil. The attack on Pearl Harbor scared people. Americans thought

The Japanese Americans were only allowed to bring small personal items that they could carry with them to the camps.

the Japanese were going to attack the West Coast. Some Americans worried that the Japanese people living in the United States might be spies for Japan. It did not matter that these people were innocent. The president signed an order that Japanese people living on the West Coast must go to these camps.

The prisoners stayed in these camps for a long time. Some stayed for up to four years until the camps were closed. They had no lawyers to defend their rights.

Spies

During the war, no Japanese Americans were caught spying. The government found 10 people guilty of **espionage** (ES-pee-uh-naj). They were all white Americans.

Congress Says Sorry

In 1988, Congress passed the Civil Liberties Act. It said that a "grave injustice was done" to Japanese Americans. It sent each victim $20,000 for his or her suffering.

President Ronald Reagan signs the Civil Liberties Act of 1988.

General Douglas MacArthur

General Douglas MacArthur was one of the best-known leaders of World War II. He was very sure of himself and knew that he would win the war. He was successful in his battles by using bombers and fighters to support troops who were fighting on the ground.

General Douglas MacArthur wades ashore in the Philippines in October 1944.

Guadalcanal

The six-month battle at Guadalcanal (gwaw-duhl-kuh-NAL) in the Pacific took place on land and in the water. The area around Guadalcanal is full of sunken ships. It is estimated that 20,000 men died as these ships sank. About 24,500 Japanese died on land, too. It was a terrible battle.

An injured soldier at Guadalcanal is being taken through the jungle to a nearby hospital.

Doolittle Did a Lot for His Country

James Doolittle led a very risky mission in April 1942. He took 80 men and 16 bombers over three cities in Japan. Doolittle's men dropped bombs on these cities and quickly flew away.

These bombs did more damage to Japan's **psyche** (SI-kee) than to the land. Japan had bragged that their homeland was **impregnable** (im-PREG-nuh-buhl). Now, the whole world saw that the United States could attack Japan's mainland. This did a lot for American confidence.

Because of this, the Japanese leaders made big plans. In June 1942, the Japanese attacked the U.S. base on Midway. Midway is a small island in the Pacific Ocean. A victory there could give the Japanese control over Hawaii. And, controlling Hawaii meant the ability to attack the western United States.

The Japanese counted on this being a surprise attack. But the U.S. codebreakers were hard at work. United States forces readied their planes, fought back at Midway Island, and won the battle.

This is one of General Doolittle's planes taking off for a mission.

Beaches, Mainland, and the End of Hitler

The United States entering the war gave the Allies hope that they could win. An important step to winning was to take France back from the Nazis. In June 1944, the Allies stormed the beaches at Normandy, France. At first, Hitler was excited about this battle. But by the end of the first day, the Allies had overwhelmed the Nazis on the front line. Over the next few months, the Allies fought through the mainland of France. The Nazis fled.

Then, the Allies sent **bomber** planes to bomb German cities. For the first time in the war, Germany's homeland was under attack. Hitler still felt that he would win because he had his people behind him. He called elderly men and young boys to take up arms and fight for Germany. Hitler told them to defend their capital, Berlin. But it was hopeless. The Soviets were already there, and they wanted revenge.

As Allied troops moved into German-controlled areas, they found Hitler's concentration camps. There were starving people, dead bodies, and filth all over. The world was horrified. The Germans surrendered on May 8, 1945. At last the war was over in Europe, but it still raged in the Pacific.

The invasion of Normandy began at dawn on June 6, 1944. The first men to land on the beaches faced heavy German fire. Thousands of men were killed. The forces kept arriving and eventually overpowered the Germans.

Hitler killed himself on April 30, 1945.

The End of Hitler

Hitler could not face the disgrace of surrender. So he killed himself before the Soviets found him.

Women in Combat

The only women allowed in combat were nurses. These brave women helped wounded soldiers. One of the most dangerous roles for these women was flight nurse. Flight nurses flew on planes and helped transport wounded soldiers from battlefields to field hospitals. Because the planes could crash or be shot down, these women had to be brave and in good physical health.

The Island That Smelled Like Sulfur

One problem stood in the way of attacking Japan's mainland. It was a little island called Iwo Jima (ee-WOH JEE-muh). The island is 750 miles (1,210 km) south of Japan. When U.S. bombers flew toward Japan, Japanese planes taking off from this island shot them down. The United States needed to take over this base to stop the attacks. Then, the United States could use the island as a base for its planes. The planes could refuel before attacking Japan's mainland.

The Japanese knew the Americans would try to take Iwo Jima. The Japanese commander there needed **reinforcements** (ree-uhn-FORS-muhntz) to win the battle. When he heard no new soldiers were coming, he knew he could not keep the island from falling. His only job then was to fight for as long as he could. The Japanese had dug deep caves directly into the volcano on the island. They hid tanks and cannons in the sides of the volcano. Thousands of land mines were buried on the beach. The Japanese commander challenged his men to kill at least 10 Americans before they died. He wanted them to fight to their deaths rather than surrender.

The battle at Iwo Jima was a horrible fight. Thousands of men died on both sides. After 34 days, the battle was finally over. The Americans had won a new base in the Pacific. From there, they successfully launched planes to drop bombs on Japan's cities.

A Japanese kamikaze pilot crashes his plane onto the deck of a U.S. warship.

Kamikaze Pilots

Kamikaze (kaw-mi-KAH-zee) pilots were willing to die in a crash. They fought for Japan and flew their planes right into the enemy. To them, it was a disgrace to surrender. Fewer than five percent of Japanese troops surrendered.

What Does *Iwo Jima* Mean?

Did you know that *Iwo Jima* means Sulfur Island? The island was named for the rotten smell that comes from the island's extinct volcano. The beaches there are covered in black volcanic sand.

This image taken on Iwo Jima was used to raise money for the war effort. The six men in this photograph became symbols of the war. Three of them died during this battle.

When an Atomic Bomb Drops

What does an atomic bomb do when it is dropped? Its shock wave makes everything in its path disappear. Its **thermal** (THUHR-muhl) rays burn people. Fire burns in all directions, and thick dust covers the sky.

Effects of Radiation

Hundreds of thousands of Japanese people died in the years after the bombs were dropped. **Radiation** (ray-dee-AY-shuhn) from the blasts made them sick.

Japan Surrenders

August 1945 brought destruction never seen before that time. Scientists had created a special bomb by dividing atoms. They knew it was a powerful bomb, but no one knew just how powerful. President Harry S. Truman decided to end the war by dropping the atomic bomb on Japan's homeland.

Just days before dropping the atomic bomb, U.S. planes dropped leaflets over Hiroshima (huh-ROH-shuh-muh). These leaflets warned the people to leave their city, but no one listened. The bomb was dropped on August 6, 1945, in the morning. People were at work and

In Hiroshima, what was not destroyed by the atomic bomb "Little Man" was completely burned by fires after the explosion.

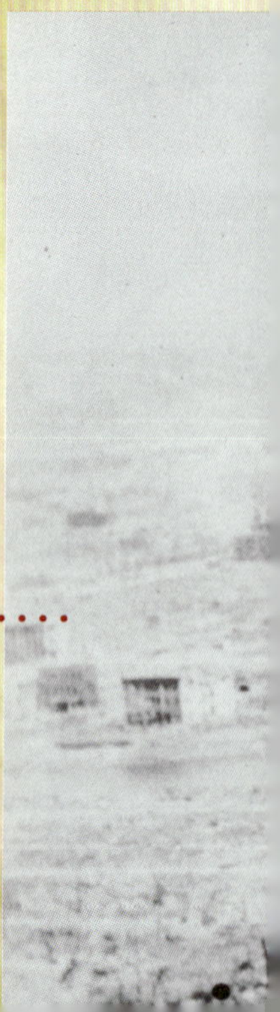

On August 9, 1945, the United States dropped the atomic bomb "Fat Man" on Nagasaki, Japan.

children were playing in the streets. This atomic bomb destroyed the city. More than 70,000 Japanese people died immediately.

With no word from Japan, three days later, another atomic bomb was dropped. This time it landed in Nagasaki (nah-gah-SAH-kee). Approximately 40,000 people died instantly. Japanese leaders knew they had to stop fighting. Their surrender came days later. World War II was finally over.

There is always a great cost to a war. Even though there is one side who surrenders to the other, no one really wins. World War II took more than 50 million lives. Innocent people lost their loved ones, their homes, and their lives. It also opened the way for making and using more deadly bombs. For these reasons, World War II is called the deadliest war in history.

Glossary

blitzkrieg—a battle strategy where planes drop many bombs in a surprise attack on an enemy before tanks attack

bomber—a plane that dropped bombs in a war

citizens—people who have the right to live in a country because they were born there or people who have received the legal papers needed to live in a country

code—a secret language used for long-distance communicating

concentration camps—camps where people are contained; similar to prisons

deciphered—decoded or figured out

dictators—absolute rulers

draft—a government program to bring people into the armed forces

embargo—a ban by a government on certain or all trade with a foreign nation

espionage—to spy against one's country

ghettos—overcrowded slums where many people live in small areas

impregnable—invincible; indestructible

inadequate—not good enough

internment camps—locations where prisoners are kept during a war

isolationists—people who want their country to worry only about its own problems and not get involved in outside conflicts

kamikaze—Japanese pilot who flew his plane into targets and died on impact

Nazi—political party that controlled Germany from 1933–1945

nuclear—having to do with the nucleus or center of an atom

pacifists—people who want to stay out of all wars and lead by a good example hoping others will follow

pact—an agreement

psyche—in one's mind; how one feels about something

radiation—energy waves from a nuclear weapon

reinforcements—backup troops who strengthen an army

Star of David—a hexagon star shape used as a symbol of Judaism

surrender—to stop fighting

swastika—symbol that represented the Nazi Party

thermal—a rising column of air caused by heat

Index

Image Credits

cover Corbis; p.1 Corbis; p.4 The Granger Collection, New York; p.5 The Granger Collection, New York; p.6 Photos.com; p.7 (top) Photos.com; p.7 (bottom) The Granger Collection, New York; pp.8–9 (bottom) The Granger Collection, New York; p.9 (top) The Library of Congress; p.10 Gary Blakeley/Shutterstock, Inc.; p.11 (top) Michael Fuery/Shutterstock, Inc.; p.11 (middle) The Granger Collection, New York; p.11 (bottom) The Library of Congress; pp.12–13 (top) Corbis; pp.12–13 (bottom) Corbis; p.13 The Library of Congress; p.14 Bettmann/Corbis; p.15 Corbis; pp.16–17 Corbis; p.17 (top) The Library of Congress; p.17 (bottom) The Woods Publishing Group; p.19 (top) Corbis; p.19 (bottom) The National Archives; p.20 The Library of Congress; p.21 Wally McNamee/Corbis; p.22 (top) Corbis; p.22 (bottom) The Library of Congress; p.23 Corbis; pp.24–25 The Granger Collection, New York; p.25 The Library of Congress; pp.26–27 (top) Keystone/Getty Images; pp.26–27 (bottom) Corbis; p.28 Corbis; pp.28–29 The Library of Congress